Arms of the Scotch nobility. ... and tables of dates to family honours, ... By John Millan ...

John Millan

Arms of the Scotch nobility. ... and tables of dates to family honours, ... By John Millan ...
Millan, John
ESTCID: T114378
Reproduction from British Library
Engraved throughout. Sometimes issued with: 'Arms of the English nobility' and: 'Arms of the Irish nobility' in one volume.
London : printed for ye said J. Millan, 1752.
32p. ; 12°

Eighteenth Century
Collections Online
Print Editions

Gale ECCO Print Editions

Relive history with *Eighteenth Century Collections Online*, now available in print for the independent historian and collector. This series includes the most significant English-language and foreign-language works printed in Great Britain during the eighteenth century, and is organized in seven different subject areas including literature and language; medicine, science, and technology; and religion and philosophy. The collection also includes thousands of important works from the Americas.

The eighteenth century has been called "The Age of Enlightenment." It was a period of rapid advance in print culture and publishing, in world exploration, and in the rapid growth of science and technology – all of which had a profound impact on the political and cultural landscape. At the end of the century the American Revolution, French Revolution and Industrial Revolution, perhaps three of the most significant events in modern history, set in motion developments that eventually dominated world political, economic, and social life.

In a groundbreaking effort, Gale initiated a revolution of its own: digitization of epic proportions to preserve these invaluable works in the largest online archive of its kind. Contributions from major world libraries constitute over 175,000 original printed works. Scanned images of the actual pages, rather than transcriptions, recreate the works *as they first appeared.*

Now for the first time, these high-quality digital scans of original works are available via print-on-demand, making them readily accessible to libraries, students, independent scholars, and readers of all ages.

For our initial release we have created seven robust collections to form one the world's most comprehensive catalogs of 18th century works.

Initial Gale ECCO Print Editions collections include:

> ### *History and Geography*
> Rich in titles on English life and social history, this collection spans the world as it was known to eighteenth-century historians and explorers. Titles include a wealth of travel accounts and diaries, histories of nations from throughout the world, and maps and charts of a world that was still being discovered. Students of the War of American Independence will find fascinating accounts from the British side of conflict.

Social Science
Delve into what it was like to live during the eighteenth century by reading the first-hand accounts of everyday people, including city dwellers and farmers, businessmen and bankers, artisans and merchants, artists and their patrons, politicians and their constituents. Original texts make the American, French, and Industrial revolutions vividly contemporary.

Medicine, Science and Technology
Medical theory and practice of the 1700s developed rapidly, as is evidenced by the extensive collection, which includes descriptions of diseases, their conditions, and treatments. Books on science and technology, agriculture, military technology, natural philosophy, even cookbooks, are all contained here.

Literature and Language
Western literary study flows out of eighteenth-century works by Alexander Pope, Daniel Defoe, Henry Fielding, Frances Burney, Denis Diderot, Johann Gottfried Herder, Johann Wolfgang von Goethe, and others. Experience the birth of the modern novel, or compare the development of language using dictionaries and grammar discourses.

Religion and Philosophy
The Age of Enlightenment profoundly enriched religious and philosophical understanding and continues to influence present-day thinking. Works collected here include masterpieces by David Hume, Immanuel Kant, and Jean-Jacques Rousseau, as well as religious sermons and moral debates on the issues of the day, such as the slave trade. The Age of Reason saw conflict between Protestantism and Catholicism transformed into one between faith and logic -- a debate that continues in the twenty-first century.

Law and Reference
This collection reveals the history of English common law and Empire law in a vastly changing world of British expansion. Dominating the legal field is the *Commentaries of the Law of England* by Sir William Blackstone, which first appeared in 1765. Reference works such as almanacs and catalogues continue to educate us by revealing the day-to-day workings of society.

Fine Arts
The eighteenth-century fascination with Greek and Roman antiquity followed the systematic excavation of the ruins at Pompeii and Herculaneum in southern Italy; and after 1750 a neoclassical style dominated all artistic fields. The titles here trace developments in mostly English-language works on painting, sculpture, architecture, music, theater, and other disciplines. Instructional works on musical instruments, catalogs of art objects, comic operas, and more are also included.

The BiblioLife Network

This project was made possible in part by the BiblioLife Network (BLN), a project aimed at addressing some of the huge challenges facing book preservationists around the world. The BLN includes libraries, library networks, archives, subject matter experts, online communities and library service providers. We believe every book ever published should be available as a high-quality print reproduction; printed on-demand anywhere in the world. This insures the ongoing accessibility of the content and helps generate sustainable revenue for the libraries and organizations that work to preserve these important materials.

The following book is in the "public domain" and represents an authentic reproduction of the text as printed by the original publisher. While we have attempted to accurately maintain the integrity of the original work, there are sometimes problems with the original work or the micro-film from which the books were digitized. This can result in minor errors in reproduction. Possible imperfections include missing and blurred pages, poor pictures, markings and other reproduction issues beyond our control. Because this work is culturally important, we have made it available as part of our commitment to protecting, preserving, and promoting the world's literature.

GUIDE TO FOLD-OUTS MAPS and OVERSIZED IMAGES

The book you are reading was digitized from microfilm captured over the past thirty to forty years. Years after the creation of the original microfilm, the book was converted to digital files and made available in an online database.

In an online database, page images do not need to conform to the size restrictions found in a printed book. When converting these images back into a printed bound book, the page sizes are standardized in ways that maintain the detail of the original. For large images, such as fold-out maps, the original page image is split into two or more pages

Guidelines used to determine how to split the page image follows:

- Some images are split vertically; large images require vertical and horizontal splits.
- For horizontal splits, the content is split left to right.
- For vertical splits, the content is split from top to bottom.
- For both vertical and horizontal splits, the image is processed from top left to bottom right.

ARMS of the SCOTCH NOBILITY.

With SUPPORTERS, CRESTS, MOTTO'S

And Tables of Dates to Family Honours,

viz

ORIGIN, KNIGHTS, BARONETS, GARTERS,

PEERAGE &c.

By JOHN MILLAN Bookseller,

LONDON

Printed for ye said J. Millan near Whitehall,

1752

4s or 12 with ye Arms of Engd & Ireld ye Arms of ye Baron. are in great forward.
1 Succession of Colonels & Pay of Army & Navy 1s Colour'd 1s 6d.
2 Signals Flags &c Colour'd 5s. 3 Coins Weights & Measures of all Nations
5s. 4 Compleat Card Player 2s. 5 Universal Register 6d.

2

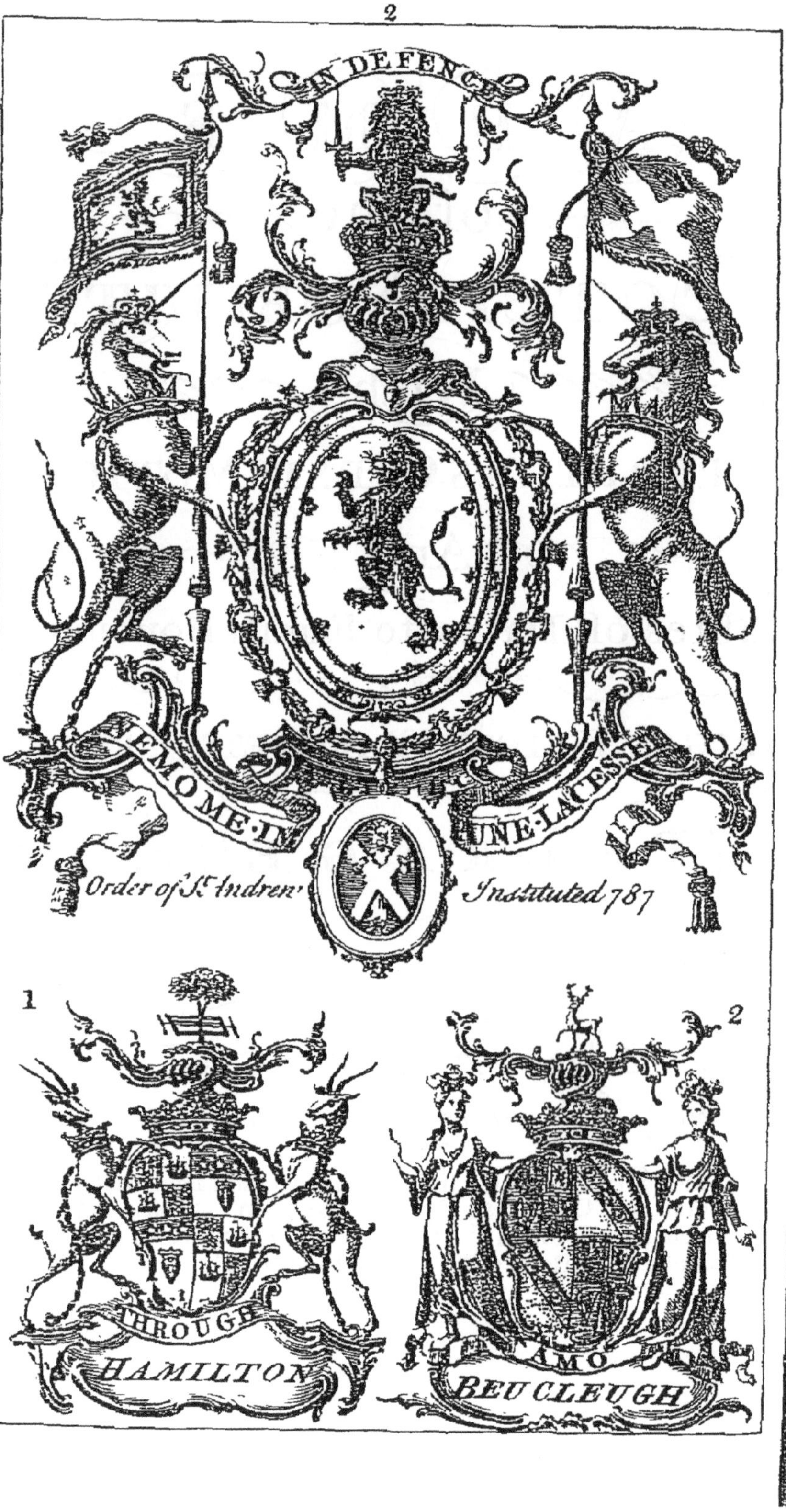
IN DEFENCE
NEMO·ME·IM
UNE·LACESSET
Order of St Andrew
Instituted 787
1
THROUGH
HAMILTON
2
AMO
BEUCLEUGH

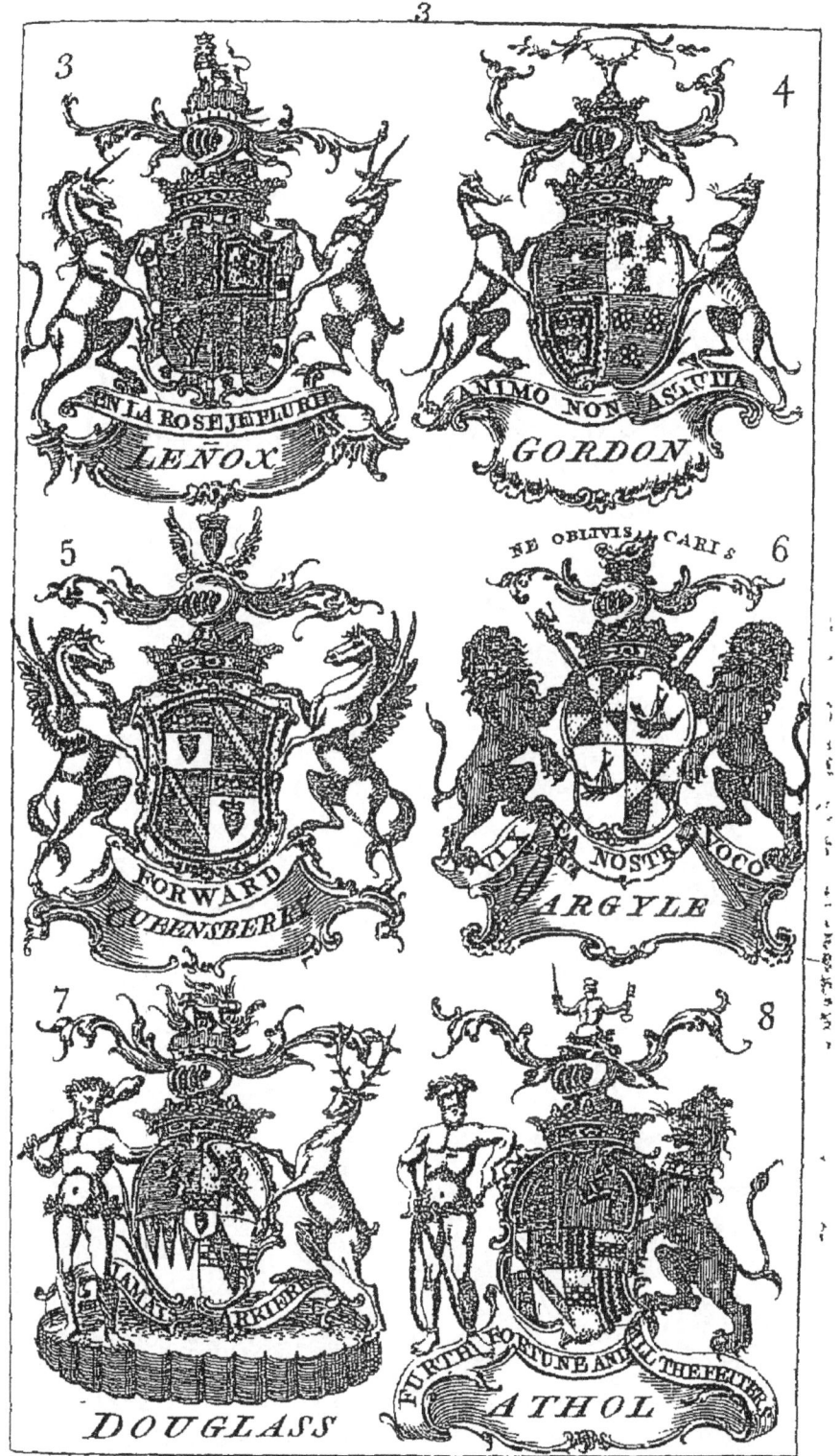

*3 Monteith p 8

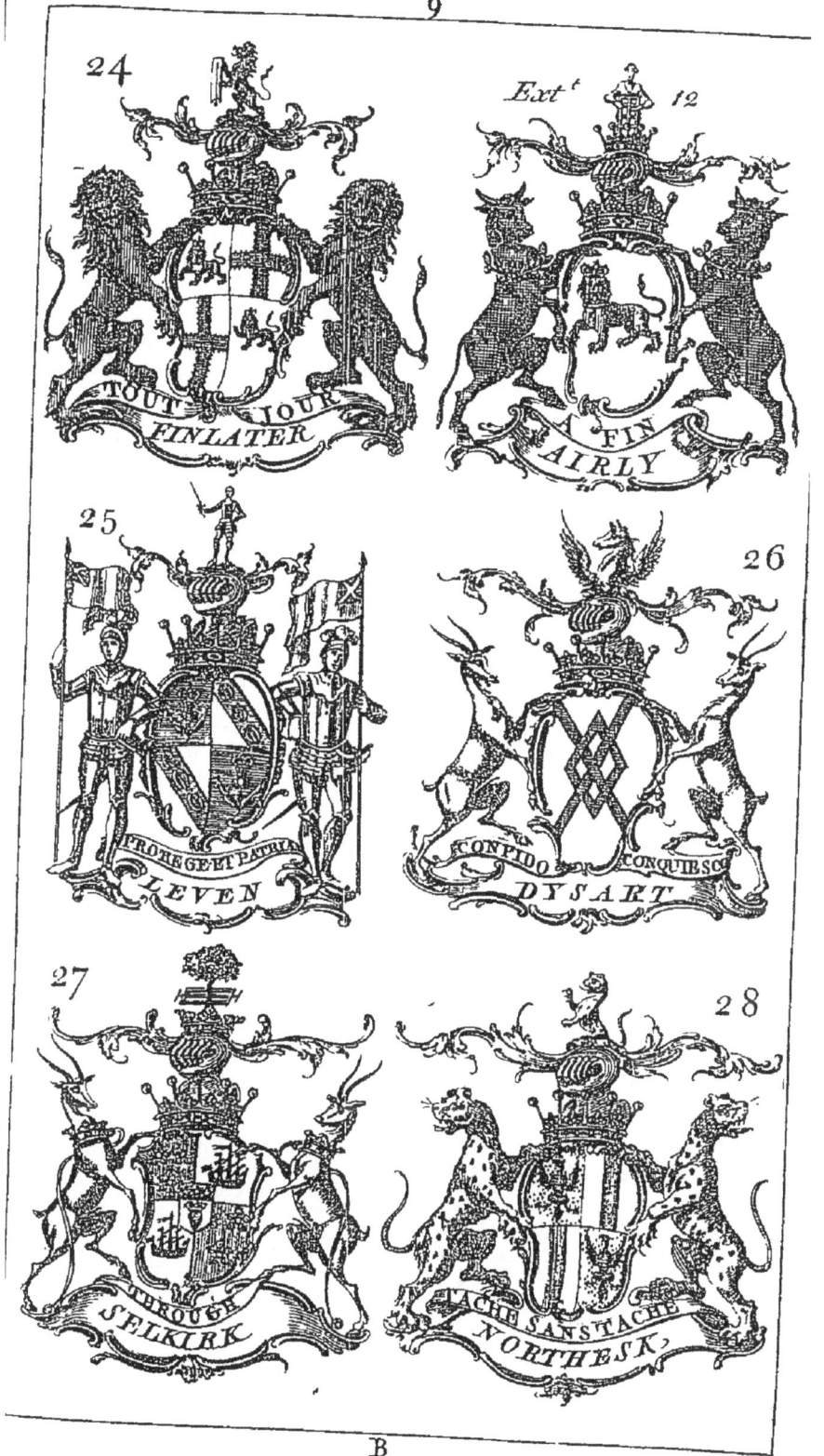

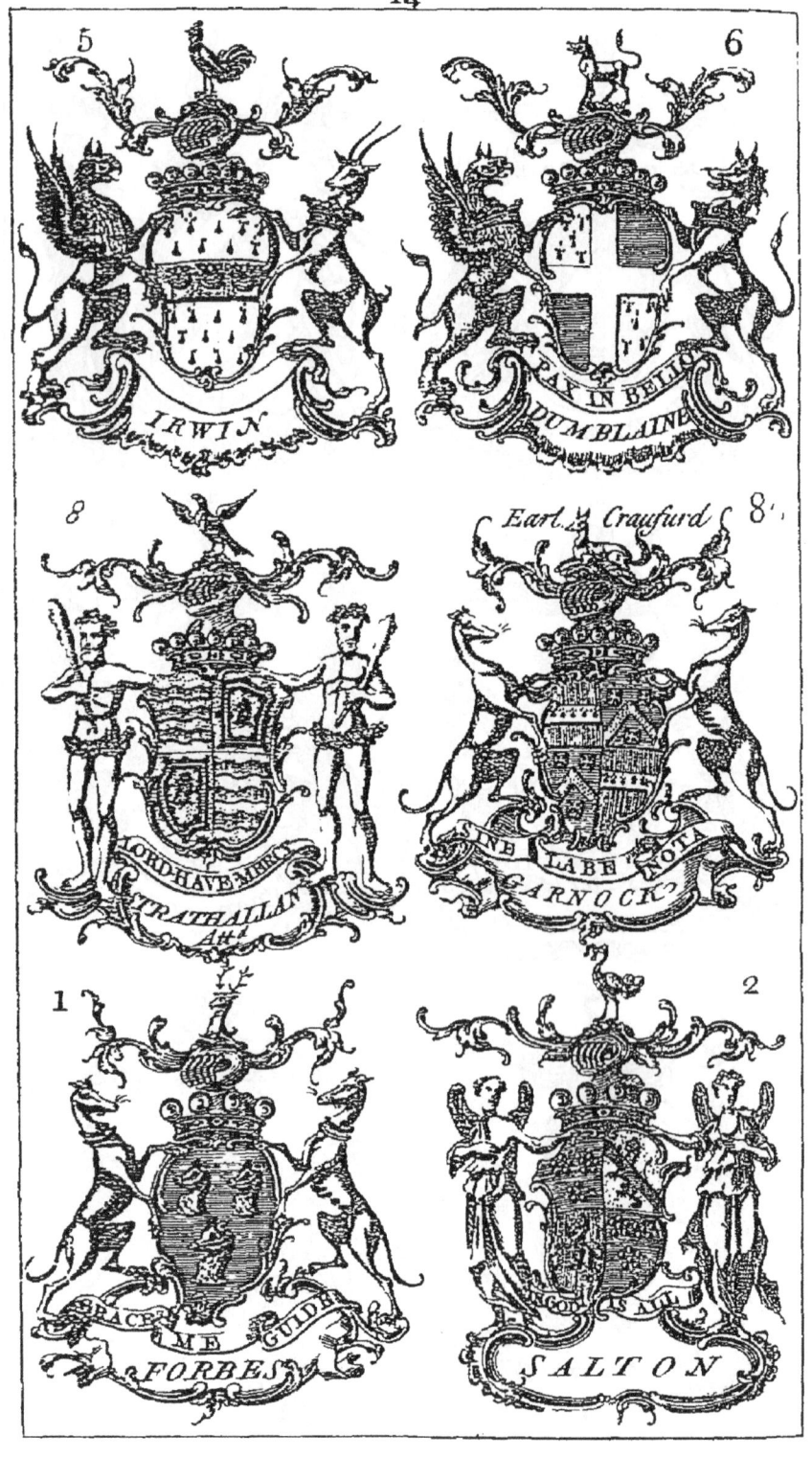

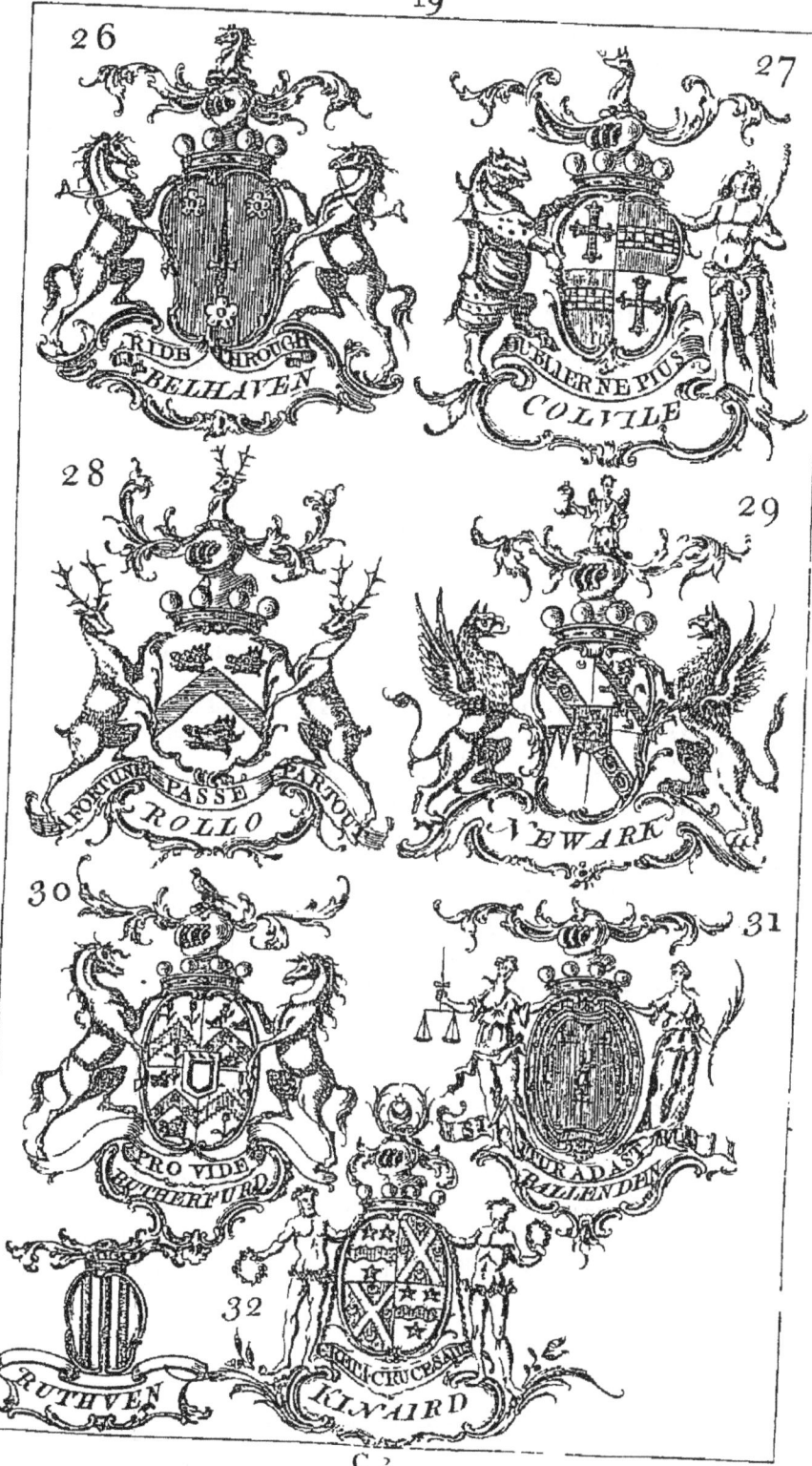

P. Wales D. Rothsay & Edinburg 2 o Steward Scotl\d voted 1716

#	DUKE	MARQ	EARL	VISCOU	LORD	THISTLE	KNIGHT	ORIGIN
1	HAMILTON 12 E 1643 f Chatlerault M 2 58 e Brandon 10 S. 1711 L. Dutton 10 S. 1711	CLYDS-DALE Hamilton 19 A 1599	Aran 10 A 1503 Lanerk 31 M 1639 e Cambridg 16 J 1619	Aven 1374 Aberbro thi 10 J 1606 Marchan shire Polmont 31 M 1639	g 2 F 1623 g 15 O 30 g 18 S 49 ge 25 S 21 N 6 F 1687 g 26 Mr 10 23 S 1726	82		1103
2	BUCCLEUGH 20 A 1673 Scot Monmouth 14 F 1663		DALKEITH 20 A 1673 Buccleugh 16 M 1619 e Doncafter 14 F 1663		Scot 16 M 1606 Tyndale 14 F 6⅔ Eskdale 20 A 73	29 M 662 7 F 1704 22 F 1724	1390	1269
3	LENOX 9 A 1675 e RICHMOND 9 A 75 f Aubigny		DARNLEY 9 S 1675 e March e 9 A 75		Settenngton e 9 A 1675 Methuen 9 S 1675	20 A 1681 g 26 M 1726		29 F 1672
4	GORDON 1 N 1684		HUNTLY 1449 17 A 1599 Enzie		Gordon 16 F 1376	6 J 1687 b 2 F 1610 16 F 174		1063
5	QUEENSBERRY 3 F 1684 Douglas e D Dover E Beverly 26 Mr 1708 B Solway		Queensberry 11 M 68 13 F 1603 Dumfries 3 F 84	Drumlanrig 1 A 1628 DRUM LANRIG Samquhar 11 F 82	Douglas 1 A 1628 Nith-to thorwald Rofs n F 8 Tibers	g 8 F 1704 7 F 1704 i b n F 82 e Ripon 26 Mr 1708		1330
6	ARGYLE 23 J 1701 Campbell e D & E Grenwich 30 A 19 e L. Chatham 26 N 5		Argyle 15 N 641 Kintyre 23 J 1701 LORN 23 J 1701	Lochow 1457 Campbel 23 J 1701 & Cowall 23 J 1701 Ila 29 O 6	1445 Glenyla Inerara Mull Dunoon 29 O 6	g 22 D 1701 4 F 1704 23 J 1701 Morvern & Tyrie 23 J 1701	1292	O Dubin D armed Campbel 404
7	DOUGLAS 18 A 1703 E Forfar 2 O 1661 E Dumbarton 9 M 1675		Douglas 17 J 1633 Angus Abernethy 9 A 1389 18 A 1703 Abernethy	Jedburgh 18 A 1703 Angus	Douglas 18 A 1703	g 22 A 1463		770 before X 230
8	ATHOLE 30 A 1703 Murray		Athole 17 F 1676 TULLBARDIN 30 A 1703 27 F 97	Glenalmon 27 J 1697	Murray 25 A 1604	6 J 1687 7 F 1704 n F 3¾	25 F 1603	1282 long before 55

	DUKE	MARQ	EARL	VISC	LORD	THISTLE	KNIGHT	ORIGIN
9	MONTROSE 24 A 1707 Graham	Montrose 16 M 1643 M 1504 GRAHAM 24 A 1707			1320 g 13 A 1650 Eſkdale Dundaff Kincarn Mugdoc		1175	General Greme 420
10	ROXBURGH 27 A 1707 Ker L·Ker 6 M 1722	Bomont Roxburgh Ceſsford 19 S 1616 27 A 1707 e Ker 6 M 1722			Ker 1603 Kelſo & Leſsmahago	g 10 O 1722		1066

7

	MARQUESS							
1	TWEEDALE Hay	26 D 1694	1 D 1646	Peebles	Gifford Lockert YESTER	b 25 F 1663		980
2	LOTHIAN Kerr	23 J 1701	b 19 J 1606 ANCRAM 24 J 1633		Newbotle 1 5 O 1587 Jedburgh 11 F 1334 2 F 1622 11 J 70	30 O 1705		D Roxburg
3	ANANDALE 	24 J 1701	1b 1661 Hartfeil 18 M 1643		*JOHNSTON 20 F 1633	7 F 1703		1370

	EARL							
1	CRAUFURD D of Montrose 1460		21 A 1399 1b 1633		*LINDSAY 1456 Spinzie 1590		1306	1069
2	ERROL C·ress Hay L· High Conſtable forever 12 N 1315		17 M 1452		HAY 1487 Married a Daught of R 2d b 25 J 1603 b 2 F 10 b 1 F 25		1424 beaty Davd	980 Germans
3	SUTHERLAND		1069 1 D 1527		STRATHNAVER S Michael Dunrobin 22 J 1716			76
4	ROTHES 1680 D Rothes Marq· Bambrugh E Lesley V Lugton L Archmuty & Caſcubery		1457		*LESLEY b 20 F 1533 Bambreigh	b 15 N 1488		Hungary 1067
5	MORTOUN Douglas		14 M 1457		ABERDOUR 1633 10 N 1738	25 J 1603		1306
6	BUCHAN Erskine V Fenton		1469		CARDROS b 25 F 1603 Auchterhouſe b 2 F 10	g 29 D 1612	1322	E Mar
*3	MONTEITH Graham		31 F 1631					D Montroſe

#	EARL		VISCOU	LORD	THISTLE	KNIGHT	ORIGIN
7	GLENCAIRN Cuningham	28 M. 1488		KILMAURS		1319	97
8	EGLINGTOUN	1503		*MONTGOMERY	b	1418	1066
9	CASSILS	1509		*KENEDY		1306	Canc 115
10	CAITHNESS St Clair	29 A. 1566		BERINDALE		1117	CountSClair 1066
11	MURRAY Stuart	10 F 1562		Down 23 M. 1565 St Colm. 1602 b 2 Jr 1610	1590 b 1418	6 Jr 1687 10 D. 1731 23 F. 1749	K Ja 5
12	HOME	4 M. 1605		DUNGLAS g 20 M. 1608 *Home 4 A. 1473	a Id	1300	E Dunbar * 1069
*12	WIGTON	19 M. 1606		*FLEMING 1436 Lenzie 1388		1405	Flanders 1134
13	STRATHMORE & KINGHORN	10 Jr 1606		GLAMES 1379 *Lyon		1330	1066
14	ABERCORN Hamilton 1r Vt Strabane 1701 Ld Strabane 8 M. 1617	10 Jr 1606		PAISLY 1591 Abercorn 1604			D Hamilton
*14	KELLY p 8 Erskine	12 M. 1619		1606 PETTEN Fenton WHIM 1603 g Dirleton	b 25 Jr 1603 15		1226 E Mar
15	HADDINGTON Hamilton	20 M. 1619		BINNING 1 M. 1716/7 30 N. 1613 Byris			D Hamilton
16	GALLOWAY Stuart	19 At 1623		2 At 1607 GAIRLIES		1306	1263
17	LAUDERDALE Duke 1 8d 1674 M. March 2 M. 1672 E. Guilford & L. Petersham 25 Jr 1674	24 M. 1624	1 b	MAITLAND Thirlestane 17 M. 1590 Liddington	g 25 Jr 1674	1330	1290
18	LOUDOUN Campbell	12 M. 1633		MACHLINE 10 A. 1706 Loudoun 1604		1306	1 Loudoun 2 Cranfurd 3 Cambel 1306
19	KINOULE e Ld Hay 29 F 1704	25 M. 1633	DUPLIN 4 My	*Hay 1627			E Errol 976
20	WEMYSS e Hay E Carlisle	25 M. 1633		ELCHO 1 At 1628 g. 31 D. 1624		1290 B 25 M. 1625	M° duff 1052

#	EARL	VISCOU	LORD	THISTLE	KNIGHT	ORIGIN
21	DUMFRIES C^{ss} 10 J^n 1633	An 1622	CRICHTON 1 11J^{n}1487	11 M^{r}1752	1306	Hungary 1069
22	DALHOUSIE 19J^{n}1633		*RAMSAY 25 A^{g}1618		1324	German 1134
23	TRAQUAIR 22J^{n}1633		LINTON *Stuart 19 A^p 1628		1405	E.Buchan 1405
24	FINLATER & 20F1638 SEAFIELD Ogilvy 24J^{n}1701	Redhaven 28J^{n}1698	DESKFORD 4 O 1616 20F 38	7 F 170¾	1405	E Airly
Att	AIRLY p.9. 2A^{p}1639		*OGILVY 1495			E.Angus 1165
25	LEVEN & MELVIL 15 N 1641 Lesly 8 A^p 90		BALGONY Melvil 30 A^p 1616		1296 b25N1488 b30M^{r}1533	Hungary 1069
26	DYSART 1646 Talmarsh		HUNTING Tower 1646	29M^{r}1743	1558 B22 M^{r}1611	1271 Muray
27	SELKIRK 14A^{g}1646 Hamilton E.Ruglen 15 A^{p}1697		Dan RICKARTON 15 A^p 1697			D.Hamilton
28	NORTHESK 1N 1647 Carnegy E.Ethie Ld Sour		ROSEHILL 20 A^p 1639		1625	E.Southesk
29	KINCARDIN 26 D 1647		*BRUCE		1567 b 2 F 1610	E.Elgin
30	BALCARAS 1651		Cumbernald *LINDSAY 7 J^n 1633			E.Craufurd
31	NEWBURGH C^{ss} 31D1660 Livingston	b13S1647	KINAIRD 31 D 1660			1436
32	ABOYN 10 S 1661 Gordon		*GLENLIVET			D.Gordon
33	DUNDONALD 12 M^{r}1669		*COCHRAN 17 D 1647			1259
34	KINTORE 26 J^{n}1677		INVERURY ib *Keith 26 J^{n}1677		K.Marshal 1660	E.Marshal 1006
35	BROADALBIN 28 J^{n}1677 Campbell N 1682	GLENORCHY			B^{t}30J^{n}1627 b27M^{r}1725	D.Argyle
36	ABERDEEN 30 N 1682 Gordon Ld Tarves & Kellie	Formartin	HADDO Methlic	B^t 1642		

#	EARL		VISCOU	LORD	THISTLE	KNIGHT	ORIGIN
37	DUNMORE Murray	16 A. 1686		FINCASTLE Blair			D. Athol
38	ORKNEY C^{ss} Hamilton	10 J. 1695		KIRKWALL Shetland	7 F. 1704		D. Hamilton
39	MARCH 1460 Beat K Ld	20 A. 1697 4 21 F		Nidpath DOUGLAS			D. Queensbery
40	MARCHMONT Home	23 A. 1697	Blassonbery 1b	POLWARTH 26 D. 1690	2 F. 1725	1625	E. Home 1413
41	HYNDFORD	25 J. 1701		*CARMICHAEL 27 D. 1647	22 J. 1742	1442	
42	STAIR Ld Stranraver & Newliston	8 A. 1703		*DALRYMPLE 20 A. 1690 Stair	25 M. 1710 Glenluce	B^t 1661	1297
43	ROSEBERRY Primrose	10 A. 1703	1 A. 1700	DALMENY		B^t	1602
44	GLASGOW Boyle	10 A. 1703	Kelburn 31 Jⁿ 1699	BOYLE			1259
45	BUTE Steuart Ld Cumra, Inchmarnock	14 A. 1703	ib Kingarth	MOUNT STEUART	10 F. 1738 B 28 M 1627	1569	K Robert 2 1330
46	HOPTON	15 A. 1703	Home 26 D. 1690	*HOPE	10 Jⁿ 1738	1567	Dutch
47	PORTMORE Collier	16 A. 1703	Millington 1 Jⁿ 1699	Portmore 2 Jⁿ 1732	27 J. 1713	B 26 F 1676	Robertson Collier
48	DELORAIN Scot	29 M^r 1706 1b	Hermitage 29 M^r 1706	Goldylands 7 Jⁿ ib	b 27 M^r 1725		D. Monmouth

Fee of Creation				Fee for the Order of St Andrew	
	£	s	d		£ s d
Duke	1000	0	0	Secretary	150 0 0
Marq^s	666	3	4	Lyon King at Arms	70 0 0
Earl	400	0	0	Gent Usher of Green Rod	70 0 0
Arch B^p	400	0	0	Heralds	30 0 0
Bishop	236	13	4	Pursuivants	18 0 0
Visc^t				State Trumpeters	9 0 0
Lord	236	13	4	By Order 14 Feb 1722/3	297 0 0
Baronet or K^t Batchelor	66	13	4	Fees by Order 17 J^y 1717	
				Secretary	55 11 1
At Funerals paid as they serve				Lyon	27 15 7
Peace in any City				Usher (Old Fee 8 6 6)	27 15 7
K^t carr. a la Baner Gold Stark					111 2 3
Col^l of a Regim^t D^o Captain Silv^r Mark				British & Irish Peers	

1752	D	M	E	V	B	Total
Eng	21	2	85	12	66	186
Scotch	10	3	34	7	36	100
Irish			38	47	34	119

VISCOUNT	LORD	THISTLE	KNIGHT	ORIGIN
1. FALKLAND Carey 10 N. 1620	1b 1603	b3 N.1604	b2 J.1610 b1 F 25	
2. STORMONT Muṙay 26 A.ʳ 1621 Lᵈ Scone Bolvaerd 14 N.1641	7 Aᵖ.1604 Cockpool & Lochmaban		1499	1281 D.Athol
3. ARBUTHNOT 16 N.1641	1b 1b		1553	1105
4. OXENFOORD Macgil 19 Aᵖ.1651		B		1117
5. IRWIN Ingram 3 Mʳ 1661				
6. DUMBLAIN Ofborn 19 F.1672		Bᵗ	1621	D.Leeds
7. STRATHALLAND 16 Aᵘ.1686 Drumond	Maderty 1607			
8. GARNOCK Craufurd 10 Aᵖ.1703	Now E Craufurd			1457

BARONS				
1. FORBES	1436		1389	1224
2. SALTOUN Frafer	1436	b4 M.1426 b6 F 83 b 89		France 807
3. GRAY	1436	b18 F1503	1293	D.Kent
4. CATHCART Schaw	1436			1178
5. SOMERVILLE Lᵈ Whichnoure 1130 Lᵈ Convath 1452	1436		1259	1066
6. LYLE Montgomery	1436		1330	1164
7. BORTHWICK	1458			Hung.1057
a. SINCLAIR Pr of Orkney D. of Oldenburgh	1489			E Caithnefs
8. MORDINGTON Douglas	1488			D Douglas
9. SEMPLE	1489		1436	1306
10. ELPHINGSTON	1509		1400	Germ 1293
11. OLIPHANT	1500		1297	1142
12. ROSS	1500		1330	1110

BARON		THISTLE	KNIGHT	ORIGIN
13	TORPHICHAN Sandilands 1563 Ld. St. of Jerusalem in Scotland Hen.th 453		1330	1060
14	LINDORES Lesley 25 D. 1600			E Rothes
15	BLANTYRE Steuart 10 F. 1606			E Galloway
16	CRANSTON .. 19 N. 1609		1329	1175
17	NAPIER .... 4 Mr. 1627			E Lenox 1057
18	FAIRFAX . 4 Mr. 1627	b 28 J. 1477 b 300 94	1460	
19	RAE Mackay . 28 Ji. 1628	B		1290
20	ASTON .. .. 28 N. 1627	b1. N. 1501 b 25 F. 1603 B 22 Mr. 1611	1326	1216
21	KIRKCUDBRIGHT Macklellan 28 M. 1633		12 Kh. 1436	
22	FORRESTER 28 Ji. 1633		1330	
11	PITSLIGO Forbes 24 Ji. 1633	Alt d 1754		Ld. Forbes
23	BAMFF Ogilvy 31 Ag. 1642	B 30 Ji. 1627		E Airly 1065
24	ELLIBANK Murray 18 Mr. 1643	1567 B 16 Mr. 1628		
25	HALKERTON Falconer 20 D. 1647	Bt 1625		
26	BELHAVEN Hamilton 15 D. 1647			D Hamilton
27	COLVIL .... 4 Ja. 1651			
28	ROLLO . 10 Ja. 1651			1370
29	NEWARK Bns. Lesley 31 Ag. 1661			E. Rothes
30	RUTHERFURD E Turot 2 F. 1662 10 Ja. 1661		1259	
31	BALLENDEN . 10 Ja. 1661		1544	D. Roxburg
32	KINAIRD . 28 D. 1682		1389	1160
27	RUTHVEN			E Gowry

PEERS of SCOTLAND Extinct &c.

DUKE		Earl	Visc't	Baron	Thistle	Origin
1	LENOX & RICHMOND Stuart	Darnly		Settrington	2 Jy 1603 2 F 23	1006
2	LAUDERDALE PERTH ...1689	14 N 1605		*Drumond	6 Ja 1687 g 88	Hungary 1064

EARL			Visc't	Baron	Thistle	Origin
1	MARISHAL	5 N 1455		*Keith		Germ'y 63
2	MAR	5 N 57		*Erskine	6 Ja 1687 10 A 1706	1226
*	GOWRY					
3	NITHSDALE	29 O 1581		*Maxwell		1163
4	WINTON	10 N 1600		*Seaton		1059
5	LINLITHGOW & CALANDAR	}15 N 1600 1641		*Livingston Almond 1632		Hungary 1057
6	DUMFERLING			*Urquhart Tyvie		L'd. Seton
7	SEAFORTH	3 D 1603		*Mackenzie 19 N 1609 Kintail	6 Ja 1687	E Kildare 1263
8	ELGIN	p // 21 Ja 1611	Bruce 1 b	*Bruce	8 Ja 1604 e 13 Ja 40	1066
*	AILSBURY	e 18 M'r 63			b 5 Ja 4/5	
9	DUNBAR	1600		*Home 1604		
10	STIRLING	G pz 14 Ja 1633	1b 1626	*Alexander	B 25 M 1625	M'Donald
11	SOUTHESK	22 Ja 33		*Carnegy 14 A 1617	1514	1330
12	AIRLY					
13	CARNWATH	1639		*Dalzel 18 S 1628	1365	838
14	FORTH Ruthven			Etrick 1224		
15	PANMURE	13 A 1646		*Maule		1015
16	CROMARTY Mackenzie	1 Ja 1703	Tarbat 15 A 1685	Mackleod B 21 M'r 1622	E Seaforth	
17	FORFAR	20 1661		Merg in	D. Douglas	
18	MIDDLETON	1660		Clearmont Fettecairn	2093	
19	TARRAS Scott			Alemoor		1293
20	KILMARNOCK	27 A 1661		*Boyd		1263
21	TEVIOT	2 F 62		(*Rutherford 19 F 1661)		
22	DUMBARTON	9 M'r 75		*Douglas Etrick	} 6 F 1687	D. Douglas
23	MELFORT	--				

32

	VISCOUNTS	Baron	Thistle	Origin
1	DUNBAR Constable 1604			E Northum 1057
2	KENMURE Gordon 8 M̃ 1643	1b		1305
3	FRENDRAUGHT Creighton 1642	1447	1124	E Dumfr 1057
4	KINGSTON Seton 6 J^a 50			E Wintoun
5	KILSYTH Livingston 17 A^g 61	Campsay 17 A^g 1661		Hung^y 1057
6	PRESTON Graham ⎫ 81	1b	B^t 29 M̃ 1629	
7	NEWHAVEN Cheyne ⎭	1688		1200
9	PRIMROSE . . 30 N 1703	1b		E Rosebery
8	STRATHALLAN Drumond 16 A^g 1680			
9	DUNDEE Graham . . 87			

	BARONS		Thistle	Origin
1	SINCLAIR page 15			
2	LOVAT Fraser . .	1333		1150
3	OCHILTREE			
4	HOLYROODHOUSE Bothwell	7 J^a 1660		31 J^y 1369
5	BALMERINO Elphinston	25 A^g 1604		Ld Elphinst.&Coup
6	BURLEIGH Balfour . . .	16 J^y 1607		1315
7	COUPAR Elphinstone	20 D. 07		
8	BRUNTISLAND Weems	30 M̃ 16		
9	MADERTZY Drumond .			
10	CRAMOND Richardson	28 F 28		
11	PITSLIGO, Forbes p 18	24 J^n ⎫ 33		Ld Forbes
12	FRASER . . .	29 J^y ⎭		
13	BARGENY Hamilton	1639		
14	YTHAN . . .	28 M^r 42		
15	DUNKELD Galloway .	15 M^y 45		
16	ABERCROMBY Sandilands	12 D 47		
17	DUFFUS Sutherlands	8 D 50		E Sutherland
18	COLVIL of CULROSS			
19	M^{c}DONALD 1b L^d of the Isles	2 S 1660		
20	GLASSFORD Abercromby for life ⎫ 21 D 82			D Marlboro
21	EYMOUTH Churchill ⎭			
22	FYVIE Seaton . .	6 A^g 1691		Winton
23	NAIRN . . .	27 J^a 1681		1651
24	SPYNZIE			
25	MONEYPENY			
26	DINGWALL Butler	30 J^y 1648		D Ormond
27	INNERKLITHING .			

CPSIA information can be obtained at www.ICGtesting.com
Printed in the USA
LVOW03s1313180214

374201LV00005B/29/P